The Ocean and I

Annie Louise Twitchell

Sometimes I wonder if the ocean will eat me.
Such a vast expanse of knowledge, the history of the world
crashing
over the rocks and sand, carrying pieces hither and yon.

It is a formidable force.

But here, I have learned that it is not the only force.

I have learned that I, too, can crash like waves, filled to
bursting with life and hope.

There is hope in the endless seas.

Friendship, Maine

July 2nd, 2017

All she wanted
was a hand to hold
as she jumped off the cliff
until she learned that maybe
jumping off the cliff was really just
a metaphor for taking a step
all by herself
without a hand to hold.

Why do the things I write always seem to come back to haunt me? I wrote Jump months and months ago. This is my Jump summer. This is me, moving myself in spite of my fear. Gosh darn it, I'm good at this writing thing: I always seem to write what I need to hear. Maybe that's part of the point, though. Maybe that's one of the things I'm supposed to be doing.

No one really told me how scary being an adult is.

Cricket loves it here almost as much as I do. She wasn't
sure, at first, when we took her down to the beach.
Water that comes to get you is entirely new to her.
Even my river has somewhere it is going, but this body of
water rolls up and grabs your paws, laughing at you when
you jump away.

She is learning to play with it, to chase back.

I am uncertain

this is so hard

explaining myself when even I don't understand

how should I expect someone else to get to know me

when I don't even know myself?

I am torn

I find it hard to breathe

the crashing ocean waves are nothing in comparison
to my racing, thudding heart
and the fear that builds inside my chest

Peace

breathe, Annie

take a deep breath and let the flowing sunset ease the turmoil
from your shoulders and bury it under the ocean waves

the ocean is big enough to carry your fear, Annie

the ocean won't drown but you might

let go of the weight, sweetie

it is not yours to carry

you were bought for a price and your fear was bought too

it is not yours to carry

I am not a hermit crab:
reason one, I do not often pinch people
(though sometimes I do, if they are particularly unruly)

I would not fit in a snail shell.

I could not carry my house on my back.

I am an earth child,
a water child,
a dream child.

But

I am a girl with words for cells and ink for blood.
In this world of paper I have made,
a snail shell is too small for me.

I touch the world from my desk,
from my log on the river bank.

You have told me that my world is too small
and now I know what I can say, so maybe you will
understand:

my hands are small, but my world is not.

I am a child of Planet Earth
and the world is mine,
waiting for me to touch it,
to claim it.

You are a leaf,
tossed about in the wind:
I am the tree you fell from.
I am not sad to see you flying so far,
but you must not ask a tree to be the same as a leaf.
I am supple, swaying in the gusts and storms.
I am not easily uprooted and tossed aside.
Do not mistake my differences for weaknesses:
my leaf, our strengths are in different places.
I will move, my leaf, but it will be
slower.
Steadier.
Deeper.
My leaf,
I am not a
fluttering thing.
But you are.

Roses and salt spray are such an interesting scent combination.
The salt deepens and stretches the rose fragrance.

The bees swarm the bank of roses that cascade down the hill to the beach. Bumble bees, two or three different kinds of honey bees – I didn't see any of the red honey bees, the ones that are endangered but I have found chasing after the clovers in our yard at home.

Friendship, Maine

July 3rd, 2017

I spent so much time on the beach today, my feet in the water, taking up space and simply *being* here. Covered in sunscreen so I don't turn into a lobster. (I've never had lobster before, but I get to try one tomorrow at the cookout.) It's absolutely amazing. I found seven pieces of sea glass and some incredible shells, and I actually did a fair bit of swimming. The ocean isn't too cold. Cricket came swimming a little bit too. I feel like crying, for no particular reason at all, except that it's glorious here. I guess that's one of the things I've been learning this summer, is how to jump, so I'm glad that it's working. I'm jumping.

The ocean is calming me.

I think I like the ocean.

It scared me at first – it goes on forever and ever,
touching everywhere.
Too big.

But, Annie, the ocean doesn't try.

The ocean flows, comes and goes, heeds the call of the tides.

The ocean follows its path.

The ocean isn't endless.

On the other side is my friend.

The ocean separates us,
but there are bigger things between us as well.

Of all the frightening things I know, the ocean is one of the
smallest.

Fear is bigger than the ocean.

If I can conquer fear, than there is no need to fear the ocean,

and it connects as well as separates.

ANNIE LOUISE TWITCHELL is a homeschool graduate who is obsessed with dragons and fairy tales. She enjoys reading, writing, poetry, and many forms of art. When she's not writing, she can often be found reading out loud to her cat, rabbit, and houseplants, or wandering barefoot in the area around her Western Maine home. Occasionally she goes places and pokes around under rocks to see if there's anything interesting.

Connect with Annie Louise Twitchell at:

AnnieLouiseTwitchell.com
Facebook.com/AnnieLouiseTwitchell
Instagram: AnnieTwitchell
Twitter: WriterAnnieLou